Juniper

THE HAPPIEST FOX

JESSIKA COKER

Juniper

THE HAPPIEST FOX

CHRONICLE BOOKS

SAN FRANCISCO

Library of Congress Cataloging-in-Publication Data
Names: Coker, Jessika, author.
Title: Juniper, the happiest fox / by Jessika Coker.
Description: San Francisco : Chronicle Books, 2018.
Identifiers: LCCN 2017025767 | ISBN 9781452167602 (alk. paper)
Subjects: LCSH: Foxes as pets – Anecdotes. | Animals as artists – Anecdotes.
Classification: LCC SF459.F68 C65 2018 | DDC 599.775—dc23
LC record available at https://lccn.loc.gov/2017025767

ISBN 978-1-4521-6760-2

Manufactured in China.

Design by **Lizzie Vaughan**

Chronicle Books LLC
680 Second Street
San Francisco, CA 94107
www.chroniclebooks.com

10 9 8 7 6 5 4 3 2

DEDICATION

This book is dedicated to my two grandmothers
who hold a very special place in my heart:
to Barbra Decker for teaching me to love animals,
and Judy Coker for teaching me to love myself.

INTRODUCTION

O nce upon a time, not so very long ago, tucked far away inside a wooden box, a mother fox gave birth to a small litter of kits. You may think that there is nothing magical about a litter of foxes. Animals are born every day. In that litter, however, there was something magical. In that litter of foxes, hiding underneath her brothers and sisters, was the smallest fox of all. A tiny bundle of tawny brown fur. And while it wasn't apparent then, the world would soon find out just how remarkable she really was.

We didn't
know it then,
but our fairy tale
was about
to begin.

THIS WASN'T AN AVERAGE LITTER; they hadn't been born in the wild. In fact, they were many generations removed from their wild ancestors. Foxes, like minks and other plush animals, have been bred for their fur for over a hundred years. Considered *domestic fur-bearing animals*, they have, over several generations, lost many of their natural instincts and now rely on the care of humans to survive. These *tame foxes* have well over four thousand genetic differences from wild foxes. The original breeders of fur foxes wanted as much fur as they could get per animal, so they selectively bred them to be larger and have a plusher coat.

Due to living in captivity, these foxes also grew to have a more friendly temperament than their wild counterparts and eventually began to exhibit dog-like behaviors. They became more docile, less shy, and more accepting of human interaction. Because of this, tame or *farmed* foxes were deemed to be nonreleasable, meaning that their dependence on humans and lack of fear of other predators made them unsuitable for life in the wild. If they had grown up in the care of humans, their options were pet or pelt. For a lucky few, like these kits and their mother fox, they ended up in kind hands, in a home, and with a new lease on life.

IT WASN'T LONG BEFORE THE KITS began to grow, and so did the runt. She became stronger every day, but was more timid than the other foxes, often preferring the company of her human caretaker to her siblings. One by one, the other fox kits found homes in sanctuaries. Most of them became *ambassadors*, foxes that work with humans to educate the public about the species. But the tiniest fox remained. Then, on one warm May day, she finally met the girl who would cherish her: me. Shy and still small enough to fit in my hand, the baby fox's sparkling dark eyes looked up to meet my gaze. Little did the tiny fox know, her whole world was about to change.

"To you I am nothing more than a fox like a hundred thousand other foxes. But if you tame me, then we shall need each other. To me, you will be unique in all the world. To you, I shall be unique in all the world...."

– Antoine de Saint-Exupéry,
The Little Prince

OUR STORY

As a little girl, I spent most of my time outside with our dogs, exploring the woods that surrounded our home. I grew up in a rural area in the south, and I felt most myself when I was in the company of some four-legged, fang-toothed beast. My parents toiled daily to run their electrical company, so my only human companion was my younger brother, who would occasionally accompany me as I walked through the shaded wood. I like to think this was an idyllic time in my life, when I really learned to understand and love nature. Even now, the wood feels deeply rooted in my being. When I begin to feel stressed or overwhelmed

by the monotony of daily life, I find myself taking to the forest to spend a few hours in solitude.

BRINGING HOME INJURED ANIMALS was something I did frequently while I was growing up. Each one felt like a small treasure, and the reward of watching them heal and grow sparked a passion in me that my mother tended to the best way she knew how. When I was old enough—about thirteen—she signed me up to volunteer at rescue shelters and zoos. Working with exotic animals was like being in a dream. The first zoo I worked at housed a handful of predators, which I happened to have a soft spot for: lions, bears, wolves, tigers, and an array of smaller wild cats. I learned all I could from the caretakers at these facilities and I constantly craved more responsibility with the animals in my care. My childhood enthusiasm blossomed, and after my first job at our local animal sanctuary, my love for animals developed into what would become an unusual career working with exotic animals. As an adult, I began shadowing zookeepers, and after working for years in multiple veterinary offices, I settled on a career in wildlife. I decided to stay in the south, at a sanctuary where I began helping care for injured animals that were native to our area and educating the public about how to help protect them. It was then that I first began working with foxes.

ONE DAY, WHILE I WAS WORKING, a woman brought in three wild fox kits she had found near the side of the road. The woman said that their mother had been hit by a car. I

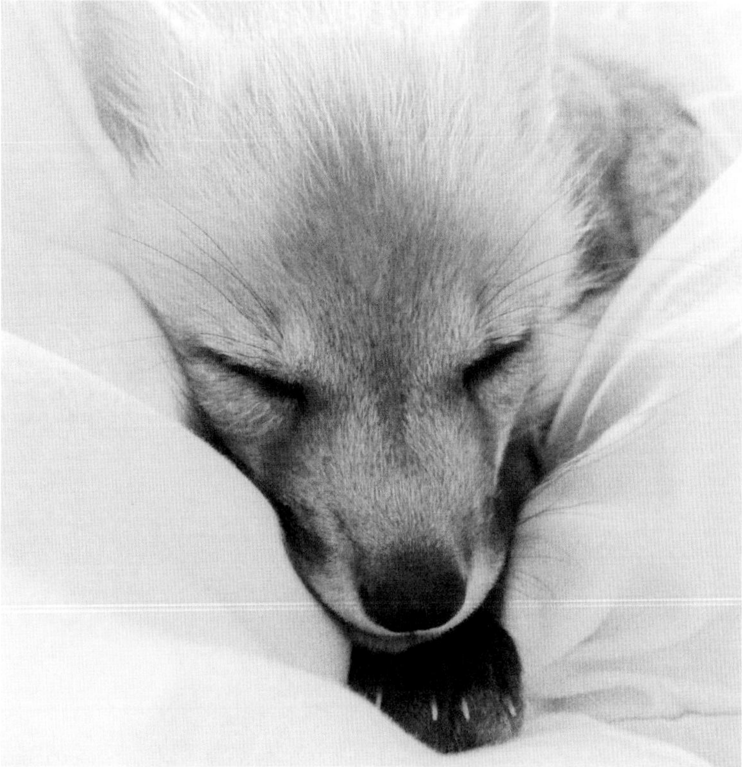

looked into their crate and they stared back at me, wide-eyed. I watched as they stumbled over one another, trying to scurry their way to the door to investigate my wiggling fingers. I could tell that they were young—no more than a few weeks old—because they still had the signature brown coat baby foxes are born with that camouflage them from predators. My colleagues and I took them into the sanctuary, and the little kits quickly became comfortable with us.

THIS WAS THE BEGINNING OF MY love affair with foxes. I looked forward to seeing those little kits every day. I was always amazed by how free spirited they were. Even the smallest things, like a beetle crawling across the grass, were treasures to them. If they saw a bug, they would all flock to it and investigate, bounding up and down excitedly, overjoyed to see something they had never observed before. They were so full of life and curious about the world around them. As they grew, I realized that they possessed something I had never seen in another animal: a remarkable playfulness that animals generally grow out of. For these foxes, everything was fun; life was just a game and they were happy to play it. When it was finally time to release them back into the wild, it was a bittersweet moment for me. I knew I'd miss them, but I was happy knowing that they were going back to where they belonged.

I CONTINUED TO WORK WITH MANY other types of animals at the sanctuary while having a few "normal" pets of my own at home. I had a

Juniper

dog named Moose and an albino snake that had been lovingly named Milk by my father. Despite my affection for the other animals I worked with, my fascination with foxes only grew after my first encounter with them. I always jumped at the opportunity to help whenever the rehab facility took them in. And then one day, a few years after we had released those first kits back into the wild, a friend who knew how much I adored foxes messaged me about a farm she knew of that had posted that they were looking for homes for a litter of foxes. It turned out I was familiar with the farm. They kept a variety of animals, most of which were from fur farms or had come from improper homes. The farm's mission was to give these animals the homes they deserved, where they would be cared for by people who understood their needs. I read through the post my friend had sent; it explained that the foxes were just a few weeks old and that each animal would need around-the-clock care. Because I had worked with foxes in the past, I knew what a challenge housing one would be. But I also knew that I would be able to provide a good home for one of these beautiful animals. So I picked up the phone and made the call that would ultimately change my life. I spoke to an older gentleman and I immediately felt as if I knew him personally. His voice was kind and grizzled, indicative of someone who lived a simple life but wasn't a stranger to hard work. We talked for a while about my qualifications; he asked if I had experience with foxes and if I truly knew what I was signing up for. After going down a checklist of questions he had for me, he finally invited me to come and meet the litter and take one home.

TWO WEEKS LATER, I DROVE FOURTEEN hours to pick her up. I felt like an expectant mother. I had already fox-proofed my home, set up an elaborate enclosure, talked to my vet, bought toys, and made a room for her. I had even picked out a name: Juniper. When I was choosing her name, I wanted something that kept her connected with her wildness, especially since she would be living such an unusual life for a fox. In Native American culture, juniper is often used to ward off negativity, making the area around it pure. It seemed like a perfect fit for my little kit. I knew she was going to be a spark of light to whomever she met. When I finally arrived at the farm, I could hardly contain my excitement. The farmer's daughter brought out two kits that she wanted me to choose from. One was a striking white and its boisterous behavior was exactly

"I was yours
before I knew,
and you have
always been
mine too."

– Lang Leav

what I had grown to expect from foxes. The other was a very tiny, brown ball of fluff, no bigger than the young girl's hand. With eyes almost the size of her whole face, the tiny fox looked up at me and immediately won me over with her snaggletoothed grin. The tiny kit had been born with an underbite, which caused her lower left canine to stick out of her mouth. This only made her that much more special. My heart was full as I scooped her up and started our journey home.

FROM THE FIRST MOMENT I HELD her, I knew I would always love her. Juniper was now permanently in my care. Hours passed as she quietly rode in my lap. As I held her close, she began to fall asleep, nuzzled against my warm arm. I was still nervous about the life that awaited us once we

arrived home. I knew foxes to be very energetic, naughty animals, and the thought of living with one was both exciting and daunting. But as I stroked her back, her eyes slowly shut, and everything felt right.

WHEN JUNIPER AWOKE THE NEXT day, I greeted her with breakfast. As I ate my banana, she delightedly scarfed down her special blend of puppy milk replacement and small bits of raw meat. She ate until she was so full, her stomach poked out from each of her sides. She then wanted to explore her new home. First, I took her outside, where she sat for a while in my lap, as if she was debating whether it was safe enough to jump down into the grass. After surveying her surroundings with those giant eyes, she finally worked up the courage to take the leap. Still only as tall as a blade of grass, she stumbled around, taking in all the smells and feeling the dirt beneath her paws until she came across a smell that was quite unfamiliar. It wasn't long before her nose led her to the end of the scent trail, and there, towering above her, was Moose.

I RESCUED MOOSE, A MALAMUTE MIX, five years before Juniper came to live with us. Moose, his five siblings, and his mother had been dropped off in front of a veterinary office where I had been volunteering, after business hours. The staff found the family the following morning, cold and wet. It had been obvious the mother was not doing well, and after evaluating her and her pups, they found that she was suffering from parvovirus. She died shortly after. Moose and his siblings, however, were lucky. They were given immunizations and cared for

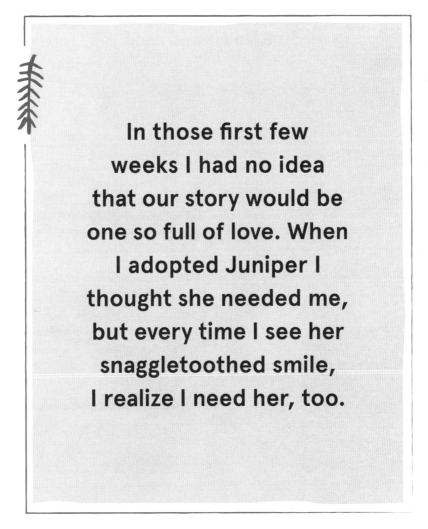

In those first few weeks I had no idea that our story would be one so full of love. When I adopted Juniper I thought she needed me, but every time I see her snaggletoothed smile, I realize I need her, too.

until they all found loving homes. I was only eighteen when I took Moose in. At the time, I had never had a dog that was my very own, but I knew that taking him home would be rewarding. And yet, I had no idea how thankful I would be, or that Moose would see me through the most crucial years of my life. He has been my constant companion and I genuinely feel like we grew up together. From living on my own for the first time, to my first real heartbreak, through sleepless nights, break-ins, and finally to a stable home as an adult, he's been there for everything. And he looks after me just as much as I look after him.

THE DAY I BROUGHT JUNIPER HOME, it became quite clear that she had never seen another animal that wasn't a fox. She was only four weeks old and was most likely separated from other animals

while living on the farm. Mesmerized by Moose's size, she stood completely still, waiting to see what he would do next. Moose leaned down and started to gently sniff her. She squealed with excitement. Confused by the sound, Moose tilted his head and began to excitedly run around Juniper, who squealed even louder, while the earth shook beneath the dog's huge paws. She could hardly contain herself. She loved this strange, silly creature. Her tail began to wag and she bounded after him, tripping over the tall blades of grass along the way. She was home.

THE FIRST WEEK SHE WAS WITH US, I barely slept. Since she was still only a few weeks old, she required constant care and needed to be fed every few hours. Between her squeals for attention and my alarm screaming throughout the night (reminding me that it was time to feed her), it was as if I had a newborn. She was generations from being a wild fox, but she still possessed some of the tendencies of her wild counterparts, and I knew that bonding with her at this age would be crucial. Even at such a young age, she had already begun to display aggressive behaviors while eating. She would make sharp noises and try to bite me if I moved my hand too close to her food. It was almost hilarious to see her snap at me while she was barely the size of a potato—until she actually did bite me. Her baby teeth were like tiny needles, and she was ferocious and determined. Since she had been the runt of the litter, she must have become accustomed to protecting her food, so I couldn't blame her for the blood running down my fingers. I had known that this was not going to be anything like having a puppy, but that moment reaffirmed it. She was a fox, and it was time I started to use my knowledge of foxes to acclimate her to our home. From that day on, I held her in my arms and fed her from my hands so that she would equate being full and happy with being close to me. I was the one giving her food, not the one who wanted to take it away.

WE HAD ONLY BEEN TOGETHER FOR a few days, so I was still getting used to having her around during my daily activities. I was lucky enough to have a job that gave me an hour for lunch. Since I lived so close to work, I would take my lunch break at home where I could check on her before spending a few more agonizing hours away from her. She seemed to always be underfoot when we were home together, which was quite different than the

I have never
seen a love
more pure than
Juniper's love
for Moose.

much more independent fox kits I had worked with in the past. She loved to cuddle; when I would pick her up she would scurry up to my shoulder, curl up, and try to sleep. Throughout the day, she would run to me, mouth wide open, eyes gleaming, and wait for my attention. She was hard to resist—she has always had this very peculiar quirk where she seems to be perpetually smiling. When I would reach down to pet her, she would yip happily and wag her tail as fast as she could before excitedly bolting out of the room. It was as if she couldn't handle the joy radiating through her body and the only appropriate reaction was to run around screaming. If she wasn't able to find me, she would make a distinct call, almost like an owl's hoot, and would pace the house looking for me. When she finally did stumble upon me, she would roll over, showing her tummy, and giving me that one-of-a-kind snaggletoothed smile before happily informing Moose that she had found me.

IT SEEMED LIKE SHE WAS A TINY kit for only a few days. Soon, her legs became long and wobbly and her fur began changing from deep brown to bright orange. She learned something new every day, and most of the time it was a new way to get into trouble. I could no longer leave anything lying out; I found remote controls missing buttons and clothes and pillows with holes in them. My carpet began to look more like strings of yarn than an actual carpet. The couch suffered the most. It had already been humbled by the animals I had fostered in the past, but Juniper took it from being a "well-

loved" couch to something that looked like it should be sitting next on the side of the road. She made the couch her den. It only took a few minutes for her to hollow out the insides under the springs and create a new hole on the side for an easy escape route. I was learning too, and her couch-den creation taught me that I could no longer leave her unsupervised.

IN THE BEGINNING OF MY JOURNEY with Juniper, I was working long hours at an insurance company, helping people with their claims. I was miserable being inside every day until dusk. I craved the outdoors and wanted the chance to express my creativity. I would spend my days on the phone with clients while simultaneously drawing and painting pieces of art that always seemed to take the shape of animals or the world around us.

My manager at the time encouraged me to take the risk and work from home as an artist. I'm so grateful she did, because I decided she was right. I realized that working from home would allow me to spend more time with Juniper and more time making and selling my art.

BEFORE LONG, JUNIPER UPGRADED from the formula mix I had been feeding her to adult fox food. She needed a raw diet like one that she would have had in the wild. While there are quite a few requirements to being a good fox mum, knowing a fox's proper diet is probably the most important. Foxes need a nutrient called taurine as part of their nourishment. I learned this when working with wildlife rehabilitators, as we would often receive foxes that people had found in the wild and hoped to keep as pets. While those people had

good intentions, they would often feed the foxes an inappropriate diet (lacking taurine), which would cause severe development issues and occasionally death. Taurine is found in animal tissues, and without it, foxes can suffer from seizures and even go blind. I knew feeding her just dog or cat food would be detrimental to her health, as most dog kibble doesn't have the right amount of taurine and cat food is too high in fat. She also needed to have adequate amounts of calcium. Foxes are not unlike other animals—they can easily go lame or suffer from not getting the correct nutrients in their food. So I started feeding her a variety of meats like quail, turkey, duck, rabbit, and other game animals she may have eaten in the wild. I mix this with green beans, carrots, or peas. I also give her apples, sweet potatoes, peaches, or raspberries. Sometimes she gets the occasional egg with ground eggshells for calcium.

SHE LOVED HER NEW FOOD, BUT HER favorite "food" of all was socks. To nobody's surprise, socks are very unhealthy. Soon after I started her on the new diet, I began to find food everywhere. When I crawled into bed at night, there were perfectly placed treats under my pillows. I found bits of strawberries in the shower drains and there were hard-boiled eggs in my shoes. Juniper had become a "doomsday prepper" and was hiding food all over the house in case of snack emergencies. I decided enough was enough after I found a whole fish filet under the corner of our carpet. Juniper had carefully removed the carpet from the tacks that held it to the floor, hidden her entire dinner underneath, and then placed the carpet back so perfectly that I didn't notice the difference until I started to smell the putrid fish three days later. That was when I began

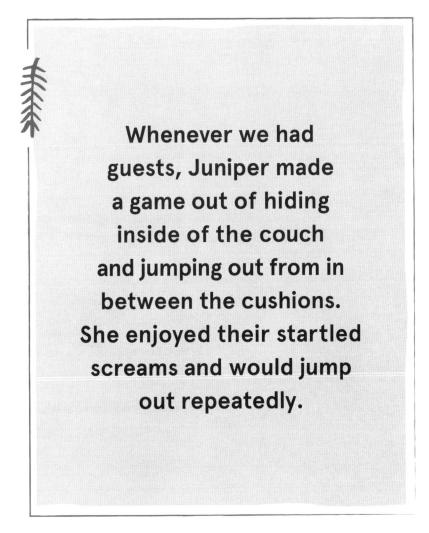

Whenever we had guests, Juniper made a game out of hiding inside of the couch and jumping out from in between the cushions. She enjoyed their startled screams and would jump out repeatedly.

feeding her outside in her enclosure instead of in the house. To this day, despite feeding her outside, she still hides treats and toys inside any chance she gets. Once, as I sat down to work on this book, my chair squeaked. Turns out she had hidden a toy under the cushion again. Cheeky girl.

THOUGH I HAD EXPERIENCE WITH foxes, I was still often shocked by how clever she was. At only a few weeks old, she already knew sit, down, shake, come, and a few other commands. She had learned to open the cabinets and she knew our daily routine—the only thing she wasn't catching onto was potty training. I had set up an outdoor enclosure for her, but she always preferred to be inside with Moose. Since she was spending so much time indoors, I knew we had to get potty training under control. Red foxes, however, are avid markers. They will mark food, toys, their beds, *your* bed, pretty much anything they feel is theirs. Their food and water dishes are no exception. I knew this habit would be nearly impossible to break since it's very natural for foxes in the wild. Once a fox pees on something, it's incredibly difficult to get the smell out. I began to notice that I could smell Juniper as soon as I opened the front door. I'd steam clean the carpets regularly, light candles, use wax burners, anything to help with the smell, but it couldn't be conquered until she understood that she couldn't just pee anywhere she pleased. Eventually, I learned that I could trick Juniper into going in her litter box by placing plants with strong odors on top of the litter. My plan began after I noticed that every time I cleaned with products that had an odor-masking agent or an artificial scent of some kind, she would

Her toy box is her favorite place to hoard treats. I once found a dog biscuit hidden inside a decapitated toy rabbit. It was sticking out almost as if she had purposefully replaced the rabbit's head with a treat.

immediately try to mark right where I had cleaned, as if to protest a smell that was not her own. Mint leaves were her favorite (or maybe least favorite) and after she marked them once, she would to go back to mark them over and over. So I used her predictable behavior and began spraying a mint smell in her litter box until she was fully litter-box trained. Or as litter-box trained as a fox could be. These days, there's still the occasional marking, but she usually saves it for new things in the house that don't already smell like her. I've learned to double check to make sure that things are tidy and there's nothing pee-worthy in her sight, but nothing is foolproof. She once found a dying wasp on the floor so I ran to her, thinking she was going to try to eat it and get stung. But before I could reach her, she turned around, squatted, and peed right on the poor thing.

THE MORE SHE AGED, THE MORE she began to display all the behaviors I expected from a fox. She smelled horrible. (Foxes have a scent gland at the base of the tail that gives off a pretty potent musky odor. It's called the violet gland and is used for intraspecies signaling and scent marking. When startled or alarmed, foxes release an especially unpleasant smell from this gland.) Juniper also began to be destructive. She was easily stressed by new people and situations, and she was constantly digging up the carpet. She had clearly begun to mature from being a cute little baby into a mischievous adolescent, which meant she had also started to become more standoffish and aggressive. If she didn't want to participate in something, she was prone to biting, and at some points I wasn't even able to touch her to take her outside. All red foxes are born in the spring— usually between March and May. During a kit's first autumn, usually near October, when they are about six months of age, they go through a series of temperament changes. The kit becomes aggressive, fearful, hyperactive, destructive, nippy, and subject to tantrums. Most days, it was hard to remember that this phase was only temporary. I was starting to feel dismayed; she spent most of her days hiding, trying to stay out of my sight. She had a special place under an armchair that became her sanctuary, where she went to work out all of her teen angst. It felt like a giant step backward in our relationship, and it lasted throughout the winter.

IT'S AROUND THIS TIME THAT, IN the wild, a kit would be driven away by its parents to fend for itself. Young foxes have to struggle to establish their own territory. Not only do they have to fight for their place in the world, they also have to deal with confusing and unfamiliar internal chemistry as their hormones begin to change. Her fear and aggression was an instinctual remnant of this. Her instincts were telling her that I was her parent, but I was going to push her away. Despite all of this, I found myself loving her more than ever. I loved that she was still connected, even slightly, to the wild. I adored that she was being the animal she was born to be, that she would never be a conventional "pet." I never wanted her to be that. Even though caring for her was more difficult now

than I ever could have imagined, this phase showed me just how fond I was of her . . . and she was of me. On the days she could overcome her hormonal changes, she still sought me out, called to me when I left the room, and licked all the wounds she had given me. She was her happy self and still looked at me with her familiar snaggletoothed smirk. On those days, it was reassuring to know that she had bonded with me. That it wasn't just one sided—she truly did care for me.

BY JANUARY, HER NORMAL BEHAVIOR had returned. Over those long, hard few months, her disposition had changed, but she had come out the other side and seemed to have blossomed. I had never expected Juniper to have such a vivid personality. When raising animals, you learn that

Every once
in a while life will
throw you a gift.
My gifts just happen
to have fur and
fang-toothed grins.

they are all very unique individuals, but I had never experienced a creature as expressive and highly opinionated as Juniper. If she wanted something, she'd take it. She never folded to please me or anyone else. She made herself happy every day. She always had a reason to smile and I envied her unapologetic nature. She was the happiest animal I had ever known.

BUT SHE WAS ALSO BECOMING extremely sassy and would let me know exactly how she felt about something. If she disliked what was going on, she'd walk over with her ears back and scream at me, then casually walk away. But there wasn't much that she disliked. Most of her disdain was reserved for being bothered when she was busy trying to gobble up things that she wasn't

supposed to, or being woken up before she had decided she'd had enough beauty sleep. The list of things she loved was longer, and that list still began with socks. After I realized that her fixation with socks wasn't dissipating with age, I began to hide them in my top drawers. I was also extra careful to keep them out of sight when we did laundry. I had thought, "out of sight out of mind," but it turns out keeping them away from her only made them a delicacy. She would knock over furniture, bite, kick, and scratch her way to them. Once she had her prize, there was no getting the socks back. She ran through the house squealing at the top of her lungs. Her sense of accomplishment made her tail wag so fast it looked more like a propeller. She'd dart into her couch nook with them and they'd never be seen again. That is until the time came for the couch to go.

BY THE FOLLOWING SPRING, THE couch had seen its last day. On the day of its departure, while I was moving the couch out to the curb, toys began to fall out the bottom. It was raining stuffed animals and squeakers! After nearly tripping several times, I had no choice but to laugh at the situation. I had always known Juniper was devious, but seeing the evidence of her crimes raining down on my feet was hilarious. I walked back in the house to see Juniper looking less distraught than I had imagined. The excitement of all of her forgotten toys had distracted her from the fact that her beloved "bedroom" was now at the end of our driveway. I looked at the perfect rectangular indentation in the carpet where the couch had been, only to see a massive pile of shredded socks. We had a hoarder living among us.

AFTER I THREW OUT HER COUCH-DEN, Juniper decided to take up residence under my bed. That was when she became an interior designer and she gradually began building her dream house. It was fully furnished with all of her large stuffed animals and stocked with leftover treats (though after the incident with the fish filet, I refused to give her anything perishable while she was indoors). Her new little hide-away even had lovely drapes that had once been my bed skirt. Her dream house was added to the list of things she loved, along with marshmallows, sleeping all day, and of course, Moose.

GROWING UP, MOOSE HAD BECOME accustomed to small animals circulating in and out of the house. He often nannied foster kittens and became a very docile and loving dog toward animals of all shapes and sizes. But I don't think he ever imagined this one would be staying for good. Juniper would follow him from room to room, always present. If Moose slept, she slept. If Moose was eating, she would stick her face right into the food bowl and eat with him. This always surprised me, since Juniper was still rather aggressive with me about food. And yet, she was never aggressive about anything when it came to Moose—even when she went through her hormonal phase in the fall. Her love for Moose was apparently more powerful than her brain's own chemistry. Moose, being the gentleman that he is, would allow her to do just about anything to him. I'd often see Moose sleeping at the foot of the bed, with Juniper curled up by his hind

The light shines
right through
her eyes, straight
to her heart,
and when she looks
at me I melt.

legs, chewing on the long hairs from his tail. As long as Moose was around, Juniper was perfectly content.

THEIR DAYS CONSISTED OF LYING IN the sun in the backyard, with Moose watching Juniper as she hunted for bugs in the grass. Foxes are known for being skittish, so she would always run to Moose for protection after hearing passing cars or the occasional firetruck. She would never run to me. He was her guardian. Most animals liked Moose, but Juniper was utterly obsessed. It became a bit of a joke—she was acting like a little girl with a crush. She had met many different people and many different dogs as she grew up, and yet she didn't treat anyone the way she treated him. Her whole demeanor would change when he walked into the room. She would fall to the floor, tail wagging ferociously, ears back, and eyes wide with excitement. She'd squeal in delight for him as if she hadn't seen him in weeks, even when it had only been minutes. I would catch her taking bits of food that she had hidden throughout the house, bringing them to him, and patiently waiting by his side for him to finish each bite. If Moose had been anywhere without her, she would run to greet him by the door, then inspect every inch of his body, collecting all of the new smells left behind in his coat. Then the sitting started. Like I said before, foxes are known to mark, but they also have a tendency to put their butts on things they think is their own. Juniper, believing Moose belonged to her and her only, started sitting on his head whenever she could. Melodramatic Moose would always plop his head down and give an audible sigh, but would allow her to continue to her heart's content.

TO THIS DAY, NOTHING MATTERS more to Juniper than Moose. However, despite her best attempts, Moose has never quite reciprocated that love. He has always tolerated her, but rarely initiates interactions with her. To her dismay, he has nearly always ignored her youthful attempts at play, but will occasionally give into romping around the backyard. Juniper is like the high-strung young girl in love with the mature older guy, who ignores all her desperate advances. Although I sometimes pity her, most of the time I admire her for her willingness to keep on trying. And I admire Moose even more. He takes so much of her ridiculous playfulness in stride and always remains patient with her. It is a true testament to his character.

AS *SHE CONTINUED TO GROW, I WOULD* take Juniper for long hikes every day, because I knew it was important for her to get enough exercise. We would go to a small creek far off of the beaten path. All the new sights and smells that had accumulated in the forest during our absence were great mental stimulation. As she sniffed the earth, I could imagine the raccoons, birds, and deer turning up leaves as they walked by, or rubbing up against a tree as they looked for food in the forest. Moose had been taught to stay nearby, and I would often let him run free through the woods while Juniper and I took our time. She loved gathering up all of the rich smells left behind by the wildlife in the dirt. I've always walked Juniper on long leads, which allow her much more freedom than a leash since

"And we'll always be friends forever, won't we?"

– The Fox and the Hound

they are over twenty feet long. The long leads give her the ability to explore to her heart's content. I usually took my camera with us since photography has been a passion of mine since I was young. I would often look up from behind the lens to see Juniper staring at me fondly, her sparkling eyes wide with excitement, smiling from ear to ear. She would call to Moose when he had gotten too far and, to my surprise, he would run back to us. He enjoyed running through the creek quickly enough to splash Juniper as he raced past her. Sometimes, watching them play together was more than my heart could take. It was hilarious watching them both try to investigate the holes left behind by other animals. They would eagerly try to crawl into a burrow to get closer to whatever animal had long since moved out. Of course, no matter how hard they tried, they could

never seem to fit, probably because they would both try to squeeze in at the same time.

BY THIS POINT, JUNIPER HAD BEEN living with us for almost a year. We had settled into a routine, and everything was becoming much easier since I knew what to expect from her every day— with only the occasional surprise thrown in. She'd sleep under the bed until four in the afternoon. When she woke up, she would waltz outside to her enclosure and spend her time gazing at the birds in the backyard. Later, she'd come back in to pester Moose before patiently waiting for her dinner. We had developed a connection that I had never felt with another animal before, even with Moose. I could tell how she was feeling at any moment and she could do the same with me. There was an unspoken bond between us, a deeply rooted trust that had developed. We needed each other. Everything was wonderful. She made every day better with her warm and happy personality.

DURING MY FREE TIME, I WOULD often find myself painting in our backyard using the acrylics and watercolors that have always mesmerized me. I've also always loved the inspiration I get from the outdoors, and of course Juniper and Moose would accompany me as I'd sit in the grass with my paints. Juniper had seen me paint many times before and had never showed much interest. It was just me doing silly human things that she couldn't be bothered with. One warm April day, I took my supplies outside, just as I had dozens of other days. Juniper and Moose were both quite hyper on this particular day, and spent the majority of their time outside zooming around the yard as I sat in the grass, watching and working. After a while, they decided to settle down. Juniper lay down right next to my portrait, stretching her legs out as far as they would go, her toes spread out, stretched to the sky. Then I had an idea. I placed some paints and paper out in front of her, thinking maybe she'd like to join me, knowing they wouldn't be harmful to her since they were a nontoxic water-based paint. I decided to go back to my own project since she initially didn't show any interest. That was until Moose walked over. She immediately jumped up to greet him and when she did, both of her front paws went straight into the paint. I suppose she was shocked by the gunk all over her feet because she froze, confused. She was still

In the woods she is
most herself and her
wild nature radiates.
With my bare feet
and her black paws
buried in the leaf litter,
we are most at home.

standing in the paint, looking down and about to sniff it, when I threw her favorite ball. I did it just in time to distract her before she snuffled up a nose full of paint. She darted for the ball, running right over the paper I placed out for her, leaving tiny flower-shaped paw prints in her wake. Excited and eager to play, she walked back over the paper, making her happy whining noise with the ball in her mouth. Paint still fresh on her toes, she marked up the paper and soon the blank paper was vibrant with fox flowers.

IT'S DIFFICULT TO SAY EXACTLY WHAT had gone through Juniper's mind at the time. She probably had just been happy to chase the ball and couldn't have cared less about the color between her toes. After that day, however, she never let me paint

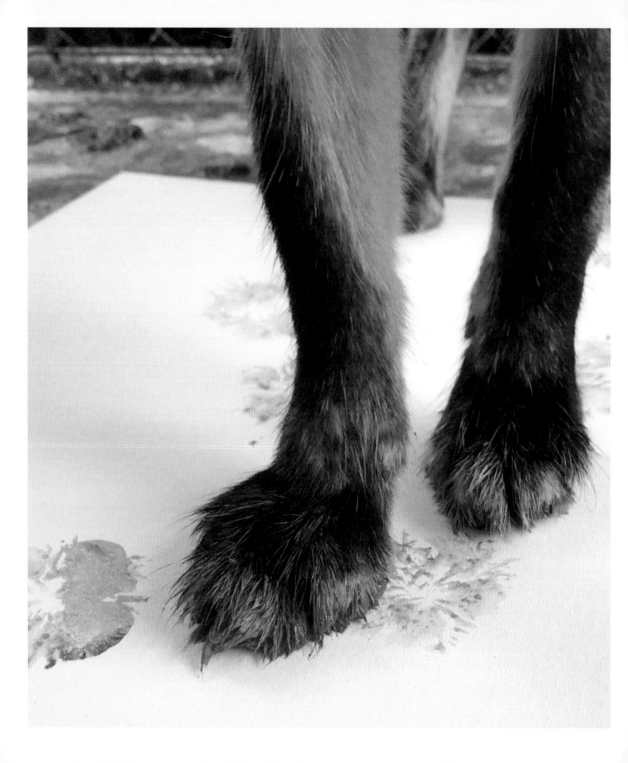

in peace again. Paints meant "play," and "play" was one of Juniper's favorite things. If I was painting, she would incessantly try to drop her ball near me and persuade me to throw it, oftentimes trampling my work and creating her own masterpiece. Over time our simple game evolved, and she wanted to paint even when she had left her ball inside. Since she seemed to enjoy it, I began laying out more and more paint colors, hoping to create new and exciting pieces. Juniper would anxiously run to the tarp I laid down and splash the paints all over the canvas. She was Pablo Pifoxso.

WHEN I FIRST ADOPTED JUNIPER, I started to document her progress on Instagram. I had intended for her little Instagram page to mainly

be for friends and family, and maybe the occasional animal lover. After only a few months, I started to see our followers go from dozens to thousands. Then after one of her videos went viral, that number became hundreds of thousands. I was overjoyed that I was able to share the happiness she brought me each and every day with so many people. I would receive messages from people daily who would thank me for sharing her. They told me that seeing her happy face had helped them fight though their depression and anxiety, and that she made their days a little bit brighter and easier to bear. It was surreal to hear those words. She had always done the same for me; it was nearly impossible to have a bad day with Juniper around. I was unaware that I had been capturing her radiant spirit through pictures

and words and that she was helping others through them. In this way, Juniper brought even more joy than I had expected. She had captured the hearts of so many more people than I could have ever imagined. They all admired her free spirit and were captivated by her constant smile. I was committed to showing them that foxes are smart, loving animals and that they are more than just something to shoot for sport or a coat. I lovingly called her following "snagglenation" since everyone adored Juniper's signature snaggletooth, and the name stuck.

NOW THAT JUNIPER WAS AN UP-AND- coming artist, I decided to share her work on the social media pages I had created. Before I knew it, I had received hundreds of requests from people all over the world. It seemed like everyone wanted a Juniper original! People were excited to see that a fox was capable of creating something beautiful, and I hoped that I could use her art to bring those who watched her closer to nature. My goal was to remind them that we all share this earth, that all animals are individuals, just like we are. I started by sending her paintings to elementary schools. There seems to be an innate sense of kinship between animals and children, and I've always felt that it's important to foster those feeling in a child. I would also send along a packet of fur that she had shed, because I remembered that, when I was young, seeing an animal was one thing, but being able to feel and touch an animal made that connection much stronger. The classrooms that received her gifts were filled with joy. I felt lucky to have her, and I was so happy that she was able to touch the lives of children, even if it was just briefly. She was making a difference. It wasn't long before her paintings were sought after by more than just schools. They were becoming very popular, and soon I was receiving more requests than I could keep up with. I decided that this was not only a way for me to give back, but it was also an opportunity. I began to save the money we were earning from her paintings to start an exotic animal sanctuary, something I had always dreamed of.

AFTER EXPERIENCING THE JOY THAT Juniper brought to me and knowing what she brought to others, I realized bringing people closer to animals was what I wanted to do for a living. I was finally ready to expand my operation. I wanted

to fulfill my lifelong dream of running an animal sanctuary. I wanted to help animals, while sharing the uniqueness of each creature with the world. The idea of running a sanctuary was both exhilarating and terrifying. It would be time-consuming and tedious to obtain all the proper permits to legally house such a variety of animals. It would also be costly to build enclosures and provide vet care, plus I would need a vehicle for driving across the country in order to pick up animals in need. There were so many variables that would need to be dissected and decided. I wasn't quite sure of where to start, so I started small. Very small. I started by rescuing one sugar glider, Petunia. Sugar gliders are tiny marsupials that resemble flying squirrels and are native to Australia and Indonesia. While they're protected in Australia, they are often exported from Indonesia to be sold as pets. Sugar gliders have actually become one of the more common exotic pets in the United States since they're easy to breed and many states don't require permits to keep them. Because of their popularity, it is not uncommon to see them in poor health since there are many people who take advantage of the fact that they can easily make money by breeding and selling their offspring. They do not think about providing them with proper care. Petunia was young and was being advertised as an "easy pet" for small children at an exhibition for reptiles. She was shaking and was obviously terrified after being passed between people for hours. After seeing her poor condition, I immediately told the vendor I would take her.

UPON BRINGING PETUNIA HOME, I realized she had quite a few health problems and some uncontrollable twitches due to malnourishment. After just a week of eating a proper diet, she started to improve. I later noticed that she also has a snaggletooth, which causes her tongue to hang out of her mouth, making her a perfect fit in our family of misfits. One sugar glider turned into two when I decided that I wanted to help more exotic animals. The more I looked, the more people I found selling animals to homes that knew nothing about their care. I saw foxes on Craigslist being sold as "the perfect mix of cat and dog." There were raccoons and minks in online ads. People claimed to have full-blooded wolves that acted just like dogs. I saw so many animals being rehoused after being sold to people who had no idea how to care for them. Of course, after the animal is no longer a cute baby, many people become overwhelmed by their care. They try to get rid of them, but there's nowhere left for these animals to go. Many sanctuaries are already at maximum capacity, and zoos will often refuse animals that they don't have an exhibit for. I decided I wanted to take them, so I started saving.

I HAVE STARTED THE LONG PROCESS of obtaining the proper permits needed to open a fully functioning sanctuary for exotic animals that have nowhere left to turn. It will be a halfway house where they can be loved, cared for, rehabilitated, and treated properly until they can find their forever home. If that home never comes, they can have a

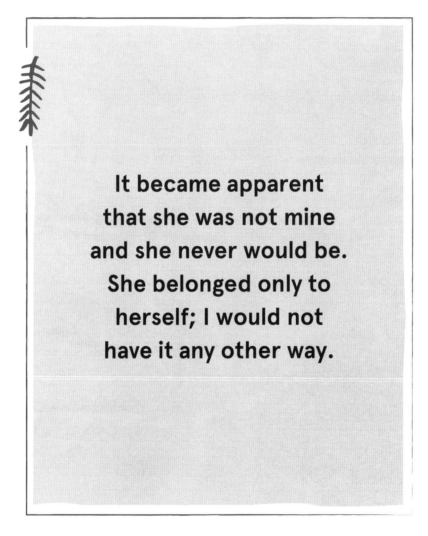

It became apparent
that she was not mine
and she never would be.
She belonged only to
herself; I would not
have it any other way.

forever home here as part of snagglenation. My hope is that by the time you're reading this, I'll have a safe and happy environment where animals of all shapes, sizes, and backgrounds can be loved and adored, the way they were always meant to be.

JUNIPER GIVES ME HOPE. SHE IS my constant reminder that there is still goodness, purity, and unconditional love in the world. The world can be heavy, but there's still a little bit of magic if you know where to look. She has given me so much joy, and she inspires me to give that joy back to others every day. She's given happiness to millions of people, just by being happy herself. Just by being the happiest fox.

EPILOGUE

When Juniper experienced a false pregnancy this past spring, my heart broke for her. Her body was telling her that she was pregnant, her instincts were alerting her to begin preparing for baby foxes, even though she was not pregnant and had never even seen another fox. I wanted to do everything in my power to give her what her heart desired. I had considered adopting another fox for the past year, but until Juniper began mothering her two toy balls as if they were baby foxes, it had only been a passing thought.

Juniper has always been fond of her special blue toy ball. It wasn't uncommon to see her carrying it around and humming sweet fox hums to it. The sound was almost like a gurgling nose that mother foxes make to their young. She'd carry it from room to room, sleep with it in her bed, and I would often find it hidden along with treats. (Although I could never ascertain whether she was purposefully trying to give the ball treats or simply hiding the ball and her rations in the same place.) She has always loved that ball, but her behavior towards it drastically changed during her second spring with me.

SPRING IS THE TIME OF YEAR THAT red foxes give birth to their young, and it became clear to me during this past spring that Juniper's instincts were telling her that she should prepare to raise some little foxes of her own. Because I have always wanted Juniper to live as naturally as possible and I never planned on her coming into contact with a male fox, I had not spayed her. Her reproductive organs were all still intact and functioning properly, which triggered the hormones that ultimately caused her false pregnancy.

I FIRST STARTED NOTICING JUNIPER'S changing behavior when she began trying to nurse that blue toy ball of hers. I didn't think much of it at first, but when I saw her gather that ball with another one and cuddling with them in her standard 'fox donut', crying and nudging them closer to her belly, I knew something was off. Her behavior began to be more extreme. Sometimes she would refuse to leave them, and often made little nests and dens outside in the yard for them. I have always done by best to give Juniper as much of a natural life as I possibly could. I have always wanted her to have access to all the resources she would have as a wild fox. But this was one area that I felt completely powerless in. It was heart breaking to see her craving motherhood, and being dumbfounded as to how I could help her.

ABOUT A WEEK AFTER SHE BEGAN
displaying her new behavior, I stumbled across a post
online by a friend of mine. That friend had recently
rescued a three-week-old fox from a fur farm who was
in horrific shape. The little fox looked like a vintage
teddy bear: he was missing an eye, a foot, a few toes
on the other foot, and the tip of his tail. Looking at
the photo of that little guy, I knew I could provide
him with a loving home, but more importantly I knew
Juniper could, too. It felt like fate, and I immediately
messaged my friend to learn more.

I FOUND OUT THAT THE LITTLE FOX
had contracted a bacterial infection shortly after
being born. I knew from my past veterinary work
that a bacterial infection can damage blood vessels
and reduce oxygen flow to the major organs, leading
to limb loss and tissue damage. This is what had

happened to the little kit. Instead of seeing his injuries as a hurdle, however, his poor condition only made me want him more so I could nurse him back to health and give him a happy, easy life.

JUNIPER NEEDED A BABY, AND THIS baby needed a home. So I told my friend I would gladly adopt the baby fox, and after filling out paperwork and permits, I drove nearly twenty hours to pick my new friend up.

WHEN I MET THE NEW FOX, I WAS immediately struck by how different he was from Juniper in his demeanor. He was very shy and quite calm. While I filed my paperwork, he was allowed to engage with a few of the other rescue foxes on the property. The others running excitedly, jumping and playing with each other in typical fox fashion, but this little fox chose differently. He found a small hole to lie in to watch the others. He kept to himself, calmly enjoying the sunshine and fresh air. I smiled as I realized that it made sense: every animal I've taken in has had a truly unique personality. Why would this little kit be any different?

A FEW DAYS LATER, ONCE WE WERE home, it was time to introduce the new fox to Juniper. Even though I knew Juniper needed someone to mother, I was insanely nervous about their introduction. What if she didn't accept him? What if she felt competitive with him? I knew that Juniper tends not to like animals that are similar to her in size or smaller, so I was worried she would reject the baby.

I TOOK THINGS SLOWLY AND DECIDED to introduce them through a pet carrier just to be safe. Juniper sniffed around the edges of the carrier, curiously. Then she put her nose up to the bars and touched her nose to his. As soon as she smelled him, she immediately began to make sweet cooing sounds at the baby, the same sounds she had been making to her toy balls just a few weeks prior. She was interested in him and I was relieved! Once I saw her body language—she was relaxed and seemed happy—I let them interact face to face. I was still a little nervous, but I took the baby out of his protective crate and held him in my arms. Then I allowed her to sniff him. She was so cautious. Fearless Juniper, cautious?! She would lean in closely, but each time he moved, she would jump back. Much like a cat with some unknown object. Her cooing eventually persuaded me that it would be okay to set the baby down. As soon as I did she followed him through every inch of the room. Taking in every movement, sound, and smell. I had never seen her this way before. Finally the baby stopped moving and turned to greet her. She gently groomed his face and he cried happily. From that moment on they were inseparable.

I DECIDED TO NAME THE FOX FIG. Many of the animals in my care are named after other things found in nature. Fig just seemed to fit. It had a ring to it. Just as I had hoped, Juniper took on the role of mother fox seamlessly. She went so far, in fact, that one night she stole dinner right off my plate and took it for Fig to eat. I was left with my mouth hanging open... dinnerless! Though I was hungry and astonished, I couldn't have asked for a better situation for either fox. Fig satisfied Juniper's need to be a mother, and in turn, Fig will be able to live a more natural life by having a fox companion to grow up with.

AS WEEKS PASSED AND FIG'S PERSONALITY blossomed, it became even more opposite from Juniper's than I had initially thought. Fig is lazy and laid back; almost nothing phases him. His favorite thing to do is sleep, and if he's not sleeping he's still most likely to be on found lying down, lounging. Part of this, of course, is due to the fact that he has damaged feet, so regular activities tire him out more or can cause him pain. When I adopted him I learned that he would need a prosthetic foot as he grew. Once he gets this, he may become more active. But even so, he has a calmer energy than any fox I've met before.

BECAUSE OF HIS GENTLE NATURE, I'm hoping that in the future I will be able to do educational programs with him at the animal sanctuary I am working to build. While Fig is shy, I know he will be an amazing ambassador to teach